Little Pebble™

WHAT LIVING THINGS NEED

Living Things Need
Food

by Karen Aleo

PEBBLE
a capstone imprint

Little Pebble is published by Pebble
1710 Roe Crest Drive, North Mankato, Minnesota 56003
www.mycapstone.com

Library of Congress Cataloging-in-Publication Data
Names: Aleo, Karen, author.
Title: Living things need food / by Karen Aleo.
Description: North Mankato, Minnesota : Pebble, [2019] | Series: Little Pebble. What living things need | "Pebble is published by Capstone." | Audience: Ages 5-7. | Audience: K to grade 3.
Identifiers: LCCN 2019006175| ISBN 9781977108852 (hardcover) | ISBN 9781977110350 (pbk.) | ISBN 9781977108890 (ebook pdf)
Subjects: LCSH: Life (Biology)--Juvenile literature. | Biochemistry--Juvenile literature. | Animals--Food--Juvenile literature. | Food--Juvenile literature.
Classification: LCC QH309.2 .A4424 2019 | DDC 572--dc23
LC record available at https://lccn.loc.gov/2019006175

Editorial Credits
Anna Butzer, editor; Bobbie Nuytten, designer;
Kelly Garvin, media researcher; Kathy McColley, production specialist

Photo Credits
iStockphoto/kali9, 7; Shutterstock: Deer worawut, 19, GagliardiImages, 5, Mogens Trolle, 13, Onyx9, 15, Rudmer Zwerver, 9, Tatevosian Yana, 21, Volodymyr Plysiuk, 11, zixian, cover, ZouZou, 17

Printed and bound in China 5174

Table of Contents

Food Is a Need

Your stomach growls.

Are you hungry?

Have a snack.

All living things need food.
Food gives living things
energy. It helps
them grow too.

Animals Need Food

All animals eat food.

Animals need food to live.

Some animals eat
only plants.
Rabbits eat grass.
Crunch!

Some animals eat other animals.

Lions eat other animals.

Lions hunt their prey.

Some animals eat meat and plants. A bear eats fish. It eats plants too.

Some people eat plants.

Some people eat meat
and plants.

What do you eat?

Plants Need Food

Plants need food to grow.

They make their own food.

Plants use sunlight, air, and water.

All living things need food.

Are you still hungry?

It's time to eat!

21

Glossary

energy—the strength to do active things without getting tired

grow—to get bigger in size

hungry—feeling the need for food

hunt—to chase and kill animals for food

need—something that you have to have; you need food, shelter, and air to stay alive

prey—an animal hunted by another animal for food

Read More

Berne, Emma Carlson. *My Food, Your Food, Our Food.* North Mankato, MN: Cantata Learning, 2019.

Rustad, Martha E.H. *I Eat Well.* Healthy Me. North Mankato, MN: Capstone Press, 2017.

Wayan, James. *Food for Plants.* Rosen Real Readers: Stem and Steam Collection. New York: Rosen Classroom, 2016.

Internet Sites

Riley's Children's Health: Eat This, Not That
https://play.rileychildrens.org/kids-club/article/eat-this-not-that

Missouri Botanical Garden: Making Food
http://www.mbgnet.net/bioplants/food.html

United States Department of Agriculture: ChooseMyPlate.gov
https://www.choosemyplate.gov/#slideshow-0

Critical Thinking Questions

1. Why do living things need food?

2. What do people and animals eat?

3. What do plants need to make food?

Index